The Rainy Day
Adventure

Judy Nayer
Illustrated by Lydia Halverson

Rigby

Level O Guided Reading Chapter Book

On Our Way to English: *The Rainy Day Adventure*

© 2004 by Rigby
1000 Hart Road
Barrington, IL 60010
www.rigby.com

Text by Judy Nayer
Illustrated by Lydia Halverson

09 08 07 06 05 04
10 9 8 7 6 5 4 3

Printed in China

ISBN 0-7578-4278-X

Chapter 1

A Rainy Day

Tri glanced at her brother Vinh, who was reading a book. (Vinh loved to read mysteries.) Tri didn't want to bother him, so she looked out the car window and thought about how excited she was to be going to see her grandparents and cousins.

"Are we almost there, Mom?" Tri asked, because she was in a rush to get there!

Tri's mother cheerfully informed her that they would arrive at her grandparent's home in about 20 minutes. Tri couldn't wait!

As Tri looked out the window, she noticed that the sky was turning gray and that it was beginning to rain.

Grandmother Chin and Grandfather Phu were waiting at the door with Tri's cousins, Chuyen and Khai.

Thunder, like the sound of booming drums, interrupted their greetings. "Oh, no," said Tri's dad, "it looks as if there is going to be a big storm."

6

"What are we going to do if we can't play outside?" groaned Vinh.

Usually the children played games in their grandparents' backyard, but now they would have to think of something fun to do indoors.

At home Tri and Vinh would play computer games on rainy days, so Vinh asked Grandfather Phu if he had bought a computer yet.

"No," Grandfather said, "I still like to live the simple life, which means no computers, no video games, and no TV, just like when I was a boy in Vietnam."

"But we need them!" moaned Vinh.

"You will all be fine without those things for one day," said Khai's mother. Silently, she hoped that the rain would stop soon so that she wouldn't have to listen to the children complain all day.

8

Chapter 2

An Old Story

Grandfather decided to tell the children a story.

"Once there was a fish who wanted to be a dragon," he began, "but everyone knew that this was impossible. Every day the fish worked hard and dreamed about becoming a dragon, and do you know what happened? Finally that fish turned into a dragon!"

"Is that the end of the story?" asked Chuyen.

"Yes," laughed Grandfather.

"But what does it mean?" asked Khai.

"It means that if you work hard, you can become whatever you want, even if you are a fish who wants to become a dragon," explained Grandfather.

"I want to become a dragon!" shouted Khai.

Everyone laughed at what Khai had said, and then Grandfather said, "Your great-grandparents used to tell me stories like that when I was a young boy—especially at festival time. Would you like to see some of the toys that your grandmother and I played with at the Festival of the Moon?"

The children nodded that they would.

Chapter 3

The Chest
in the Attic

Grandfather and the children climbed the creaky steps into the attic of the two-story house. When Grandfather pulled out an old dusty toy chest, the children didn't think there would be anything exciting inside. But they were respectful of their grandfather and watched what he was doing.

Grandfather looked at his watch and then at the children and said, "I think that I'd better go downstairs and help your grandmother with dinner. You can open this chest yourselves and see what's inside."

The children waited until their grandfather left the attic, then opened the chest. Inside the chest they found a lion mask, a paper light shaped like a star, a wooden drum, and a small clay dragon. Chuyen put on the mask and roared playfully while Khai played the drum loudly.

Carefully Tri picked up the dragon and inspected it. "This is like the dragon from Grandfather's story," she said.

"These old toys are OK," said Vinh, "but what are we going to do *now?*"

Vinh, Chuyen, and Khai put the
toys back into the chest. Just as Tri
was about to put back the dragon, she
noticed a small hole in the dragon's
tail. It was a whistle! When Tri put
the whistle to her mouth and blew, a
lovely song came out. At the same
time, the little dragon toy began to
breathe out puffy clouds of white
smoke!

"What's happening?" cried Vinh.

Suddenly a rush of wind came through the attic. The wind wooshed in their ears and blew in little circles around each of them, and the children felt as if they were spinning around and around through a tunnel.

Chapter 4

A Strange and Wonderful Place

Just as suddenly as the wind began blowing, it stopped, and everything was quiet for a moment. The children could tell that they were not at their grandparent's house anymore. They were not sure where they were because they could hardly see anything except for the green walls around them.

"Where are we?" cried Chuyen.

"Sshhh, I think somebody is coming," whispered Tri.

They heard the sound of happy laughing voices getting louder and louder. Suddenly a boy and a girl wearing fine silk clothing walked in.

"Who are you?" asked the boy and girl.

"We're Tri, Vinh, Chuyen, and Khai," answered Tri. "Can you tell us where we are, and who *you* are?"

The boy said, "I'm Phu, this is Chin, and we are inside the dragon at the Moon Festival. Why are you dressed so strangely?"

The children looked at each other and all began talking at once.

"Phu and Chin are our grandparents' names!" said Chuyen to Tri.

"How can we be inside a dragon?" asked Khai.

"What do you mean we're dressed strangely?" asked Vinh.

Before any of their questions could be answered, the music began, and the children heard drums and bells.

"The parade is about to start!" shouted Chin. "Come over here and hold on!"

The children rushed to where Chin was, and held on to poles made from bamboo.

"You see," said Phu, laughing, "we're inside a dragon! These poles hold the dragon up and move it around."

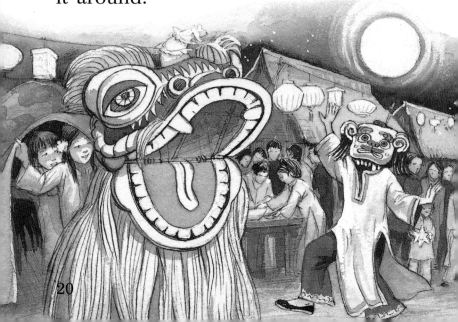

20

Chin lifted up the flap where she and Phu had entered and asked, "Do you want to see the festival?"

The children looked out of the dragon and saw that it was nighttime and that the sky was glowing with a full moon. The street was full of Vietnamese children holding little paper lights. There were people eating, dancing, and wearing animal masks of all kinds. The children thought it was the most beautiful sight they'd ever seen!

"Our village is small," said Phu, "but our festival is one of the best in Vietnam."

"Vietnam?" cried all four children at once.

Suddenly the floor began to shake, and then it rumbled as if there might be an earthquake. Luckily, they were hanging on like Chin told them to.

"The dragon is being lifted, and the dragon dance is starting," shouted Phu. "We love the movement, so every year we come inside the dragon to feel it dance!"

The children held on as the dragon went down the busy streets and moved to the beat of the music. They could hear the laughter, cheers, and claps of the crowd outside.

When the parade was over, Chin and Phu told the children to follow them. They slipped out of the dragon and walked to the middle of the village, stopping at a table on the street where Chin and Phu got toys for everyone.

Phu explained that all children get lots of toys at festival time. Chuyen got a lion's mask, Khai got a drum, Vinh got a star-shaped light, and Tri got a dragon whistle. The children were surprised because they were the same toys that each of them had taken out of the chest in Grandfather's attic!

They walked down the busy street and tried the special foods and sweets at the festival. The children were enjoying the party so much that they didn't want it to end!

Then Tri began to worry. "If we *are* in Vietnam, how will we get back to Grandfather's house?" she asked nervously.

Chapter 5

Going Back Home

Just then, Chuyen remembered how they had gotten to Vietnam in the first place. She looked at Tri, who was holding the dragon whistle. The rest of them were holding the other toys from Grandfather's box.

"Tri, I think that if you blow the dragon whistle again, we'll be able to go home," suggested Chuyen. The children thanked Phu and Chin before Tri put the whistle to her lips.

Tri blew the whistle as hard as she could. Instantly, it was dark, and the wind began to blow again. Clouds formed all around them, and the children were taken back to their grandparents' dusty attic.

They all began talking at once. Did it really happen? Wasn't it strange that the children they met had the same names as their grandparents'? How did the toys from Grandfather's chest appear at the festival?

Tri said that Grandfather
must have known that this
would happen, and that was why he
had left them alone with the chest.

"Wow!" said Vinh. "I can't
believe Grandfather knew about
that neat trip!"

Then the adults called for them to
come downstairs for dinner, so the
children returned the toys, closed the
chest, and went downstairs.

Vinh's mom said, "You were in the
attic for such a long time, I was
beginning to wonder what you were
doing up there. Grandfather's toys
couldn't have been *that* much fun."

The children smiled and looked at their grandfather, who was smiling, too.

Tri said, "Oh, the toys were better than we could have ever imagined they would be!"

Chapter 6

A Festival for Today

"Is there a Moon Festival here?" Tri asked Grandfather during dinner.

"Some Vietnamese communities in the United States have one, but we don't have one here."

"Maybe we could start a festival in our town," said Vinh. "We could make paper lights, masks, and toys!"

"I'll bet there is a lot of information on the Internet," said Khai.

"It will be a lot of work," said Grandmother.

"That's OK," said Khai. "If you work hard enough, you can get what you want. You can even become a dragon!"

Everyone smiled and agreed to help.

After dinner the rain stopped, and the skies cleared up.

"Look!" said Grandmother Chin. "You children can finally go play outside!"

"I think that we've had enough fun for one day," said Tri.

The children's parents were surprised that they didn't want to go outside, but their grandfather was not. He knew that his grandchildren had experienced something that day much more fantastic than playing outside.